START OF SOMETHING NEW

Words and Music by MATTHEW GERRARD
and ROBBIE NEVIL

Dsus2

Male: Now who'd -'ve ev - er thought ___ that

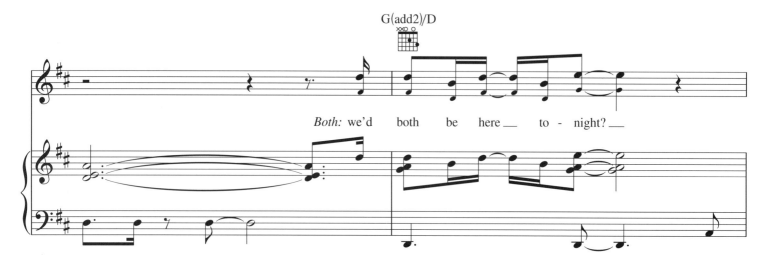

G(add2)/D

Both: we'd both be here ___ to - night? ___

D(add 2)

Female: Yeah, ___ and the world ___ looks so much bright - er, oh, ___ with you

G(add2)/D

C

D.S. al Coda

by my ___ side. ___ *Both:* I

CODA

the start of some-thing new. _____ *Male:* I nev-er knew that it could

hap-pen till it hap-pened to me. _____ Oh, _____ yeah. _____

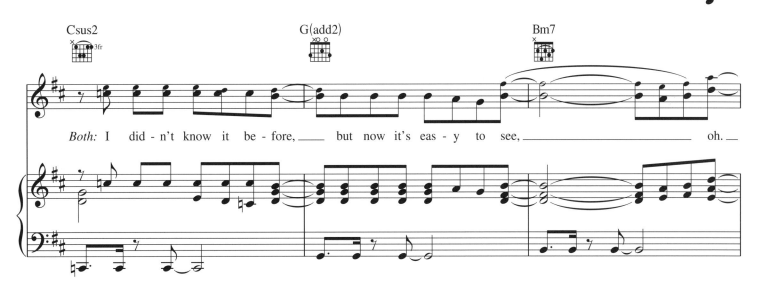

Both: I did-n't know it be-fore, _____ but now it's eas-y to see, _____ oh. _____

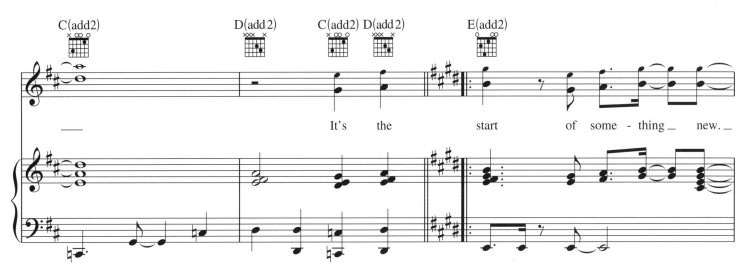

It's the start of some-thing _ new. _

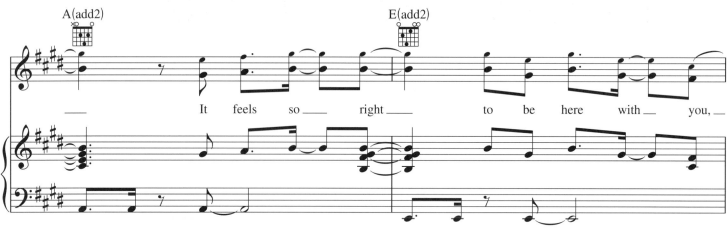

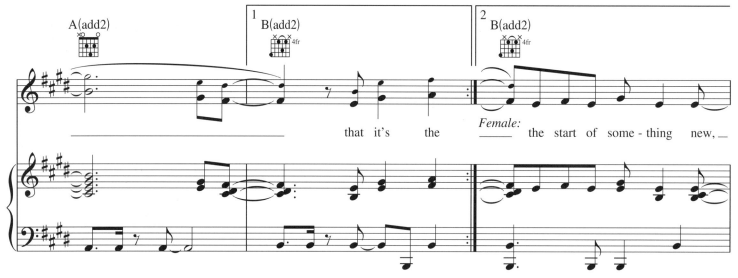

GET'CHA HEAD IN THE GAME

Words and Music by RAY CHAM,
GREG CHAM and ANDREW SEELEY

Coach said to

fake right   and break left.   Watch out for the pick and keep and eye on de-fense.   Got-ta

*Recorded a half step higher.

make sure that we get the re - bound, 'cause when we get it, then the crowd will go __ wild.

A sec - ond chance, got - ta grab it and go. _____

May - be this time, we'll hit __ the right notes. _____

Wait a min - ute; not the time or place. _ Wait a min - ute; get my head in the game. _

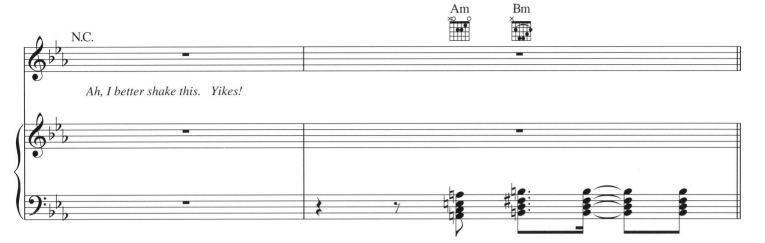

Ah, I better shake this.   Yikes!

D.S. al Coda

I   got - ta

CODA

get - 'cha,   get - 'cha,   get - 'cha,   get - 'cha   head   in   the   game. __   Whoo!) __

WHAT I'VE BEEN LOOKING FOR

Words and Music by ANDY DODD
and ADAM WATTS

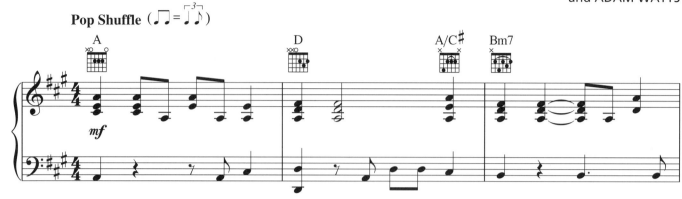

Male: It's hard to be-lieve ___ that I could-n't see ___

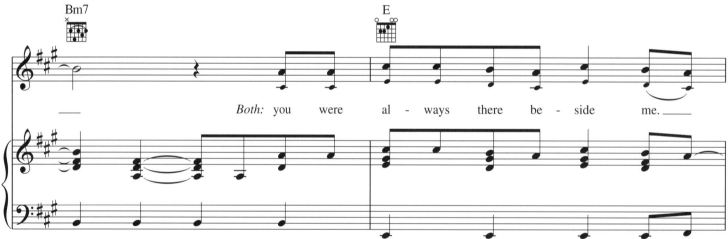

Both: you were al-ways there be-side me. ___

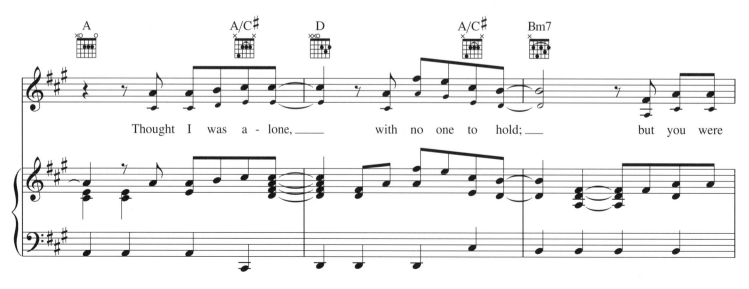

Thought I was a-lone, ___ with no one to hold; ___ but you were

al - ways there be - side me.___ *Female:* This feel - ing's like no oth - er.___

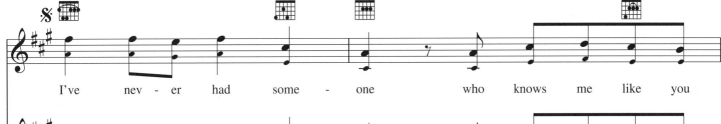

Both: I want you to know: _____

I've nev - er had some - one who knows me like you

do, ___ the way you do. _____ I've nev - er had some -

one as good for me as you; __ no one like you. __

So lone - ly be - fore; __ I fi - nal - ly found __

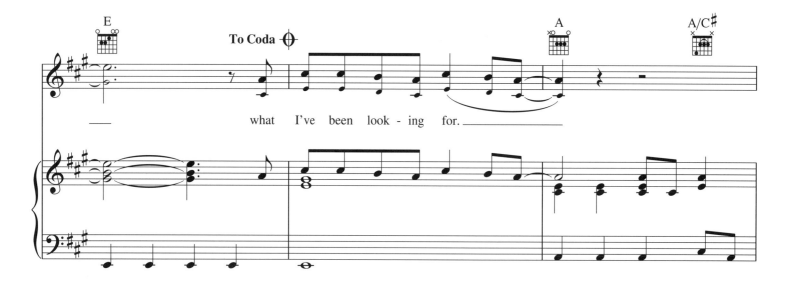

__ what I've been look - ing for. __

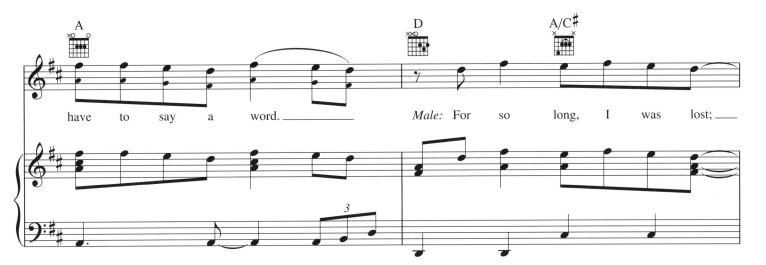

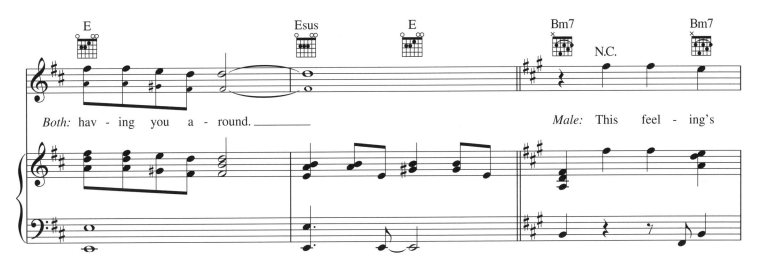

D.S. al Coda

like no oth - er. _____ *Both:* I want you to know: _____

CODA

I've been look - ing for. _____ Doo doo doo, doo doo doo doo doo

doo; a - whoa, oh, oh, oh. _____ whoa, oh, oh, oh. _____

STICK TO THE STATUS QUO

Words and Music by DAVID N. LAWRENCE
and FAYE GREENBERG

*Recorded a half step higher.

Jocks: No, no, __ no, no! __
Brainiacs: No, no, __ no, no! __
No, __ no, no; __
stick __

__ to the stuff __ you know. __

If you wan - na be cool, __ fol - low one __
It is bet - ter by far __ to keep things __

__ sim - ple rule; __ don't mess __
__ as they are. __ Don't mess __
with the flow, __ no, no. __
Stick __

__ to the sta - tus quo!

Skaterdude: Lis - ten well! I'm read - y to tell a - bout a need that I can - not de - ny. ___

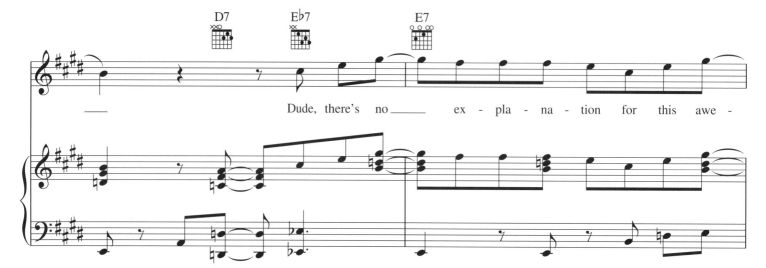

___ Dude, there's no ___ ex - pla - na - tion for this awe -

- some sen - sa - tion, but I'm read - y to ___ let ___ it ___ fly. ___

___ *Dudes & Dudettes:* Speak ___ your ___ mind, ___ and ___ you'll ___ be ___ heard. ___

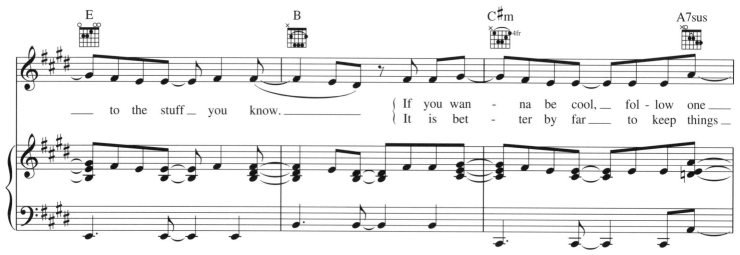

to the stuff you know. _____

If you wan - na be cool, _ fol - low one _____
It is bet - ter by far _____ to keep things _

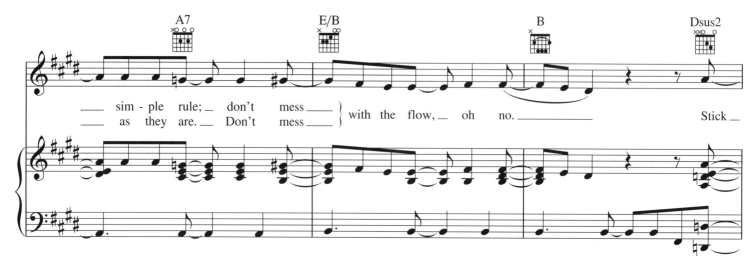

sim - ple rule; _ don't mess _____
as they are. _ Don't mess _____
with the flow, _ oh no. _____

Stick _

to the sta - tus quo. _____

_____ to the sta - tus quo!

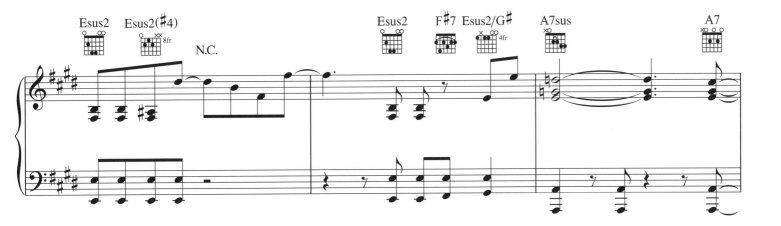

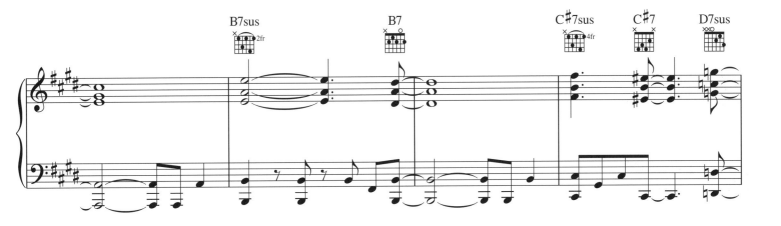

Sharpay: This is

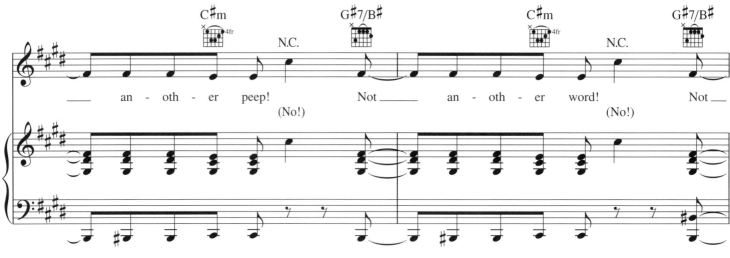

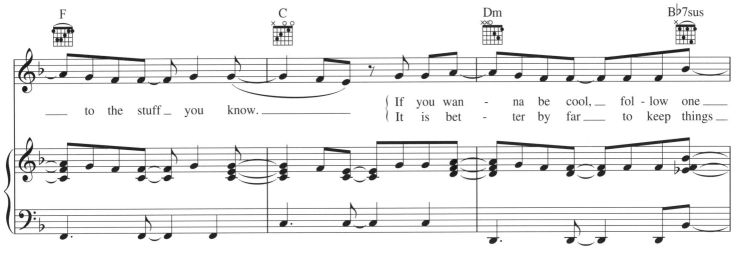

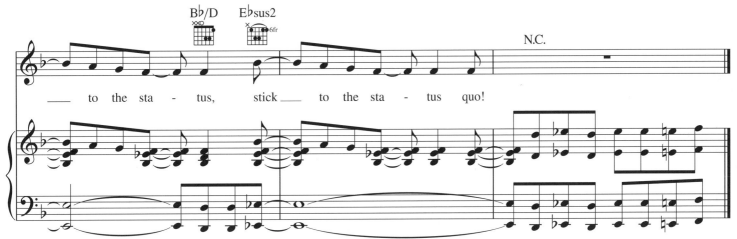

WHEN THERE WAS ME AND YOU

Words and Music by
JAMIE HOUSTON

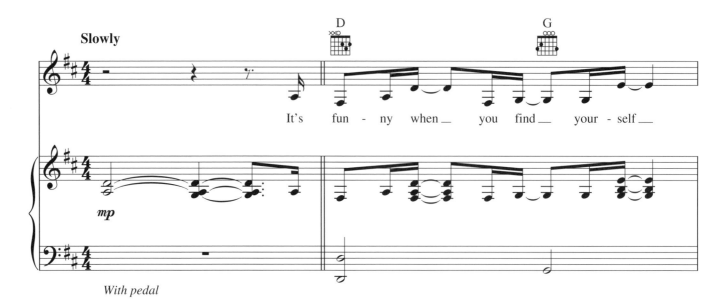

It's fun-ny when _ you find _ your-self _

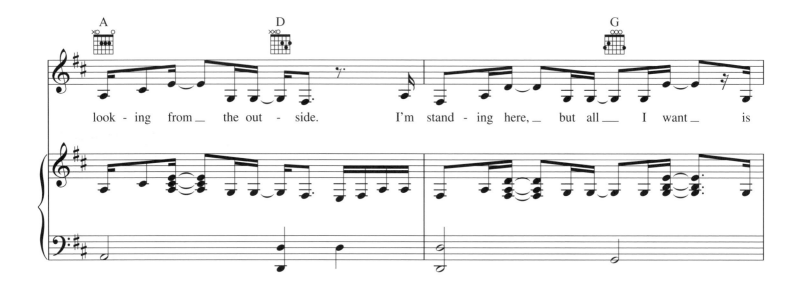

look-ing from _ the out - side. I'm stand-ing here, _ but all _ I want _ is

to be o - ver there. _____ Why did _____ I let _ my-self _ be - lieve _

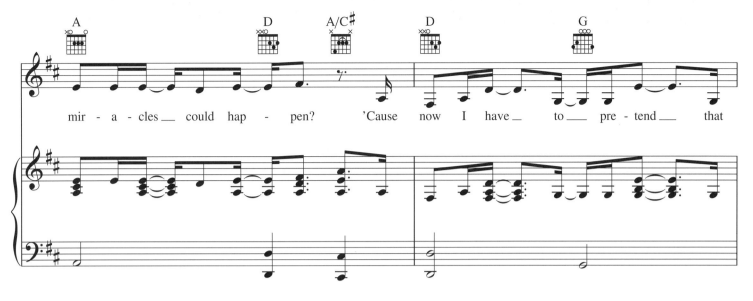

mir - a - cles___ could hap - pen? 'Cause now I have___ to___ pre - tend___ that

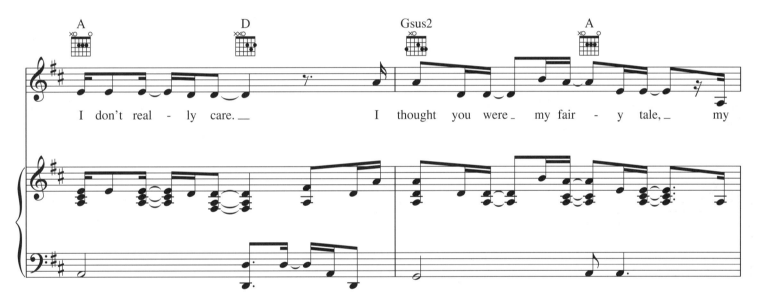

I don't real - ly care.___ I thought you were___ my fair - y tale,___ my

dream___ when I'm___ not sleep - ing, a wish up - on___ a star___ that's com - ing true.___

But ev-'ry-bod-y else __ could tell __ that

I con-fused __ my feel-ings with __ the truth, ___ when there was me __ and you. __

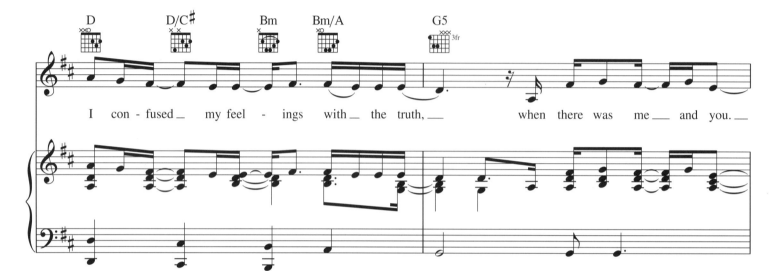

__ I swore I knew __ the mel-o-dy

that I heard __ you sing-ing. And when you smiled, __ you made __ me feel __ like

I could sing a - long. But then

you went and changed the words; now my heart is emp - ty. I'm

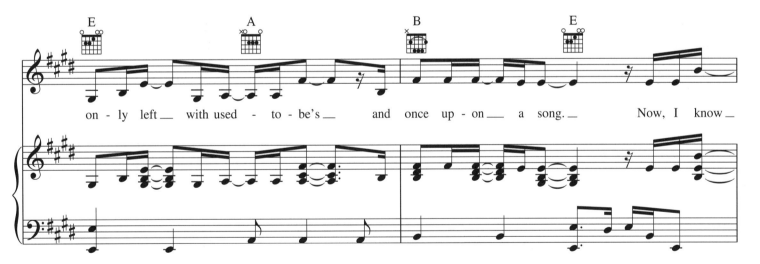

on - ly left with used - to - be's and once up - on a song. Now, I know

you're not a fair - y tale, and dreams were meant for sleep - ing, and

wish - es on a star __ just don't come true. _____ 'Cause now, __

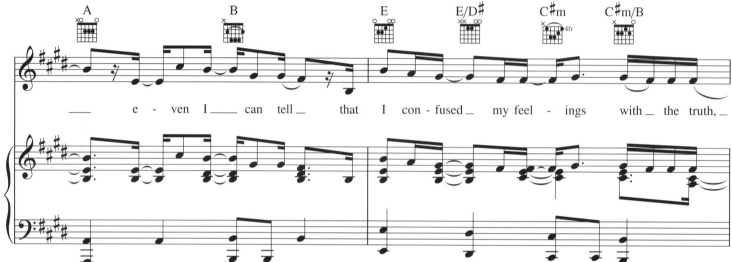

__ e - ven I __ can tell __ that I con - fused __ my feel - ings with __ the truth, __

__ be - cause I liked __ the view _____ when there __ was me __ and you. __

__ I can't be - lieve __ that I could be __ so blind. __ It's like you were float -

BOP TO THE TOP

Words and Music by RANDY PETERSEN
and KEVIN QUINN

shoot-ing for ___ the stars. ___ *Male:* Ba - by, to ___ be num - ber one, ___ you've

got to raise ___ the bar. ___ *Female:* A - kick - in' and ___ a-scratch - in', ___

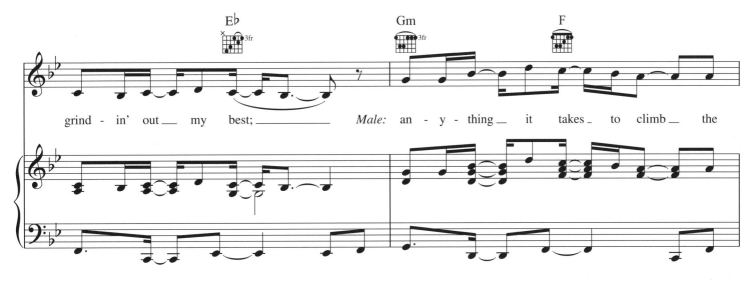

grind - in' out ___ my best; ___ *Male:* an - y - thing ___ it takes ___ to climb ___ the

lad - der of ___ suc - cess. *Both:* Work our tails ___ off ev - 'ry day; ___

we got-ta bump the com-pe-ti-tion, blow them all a-way. ____

Male: Caliente! *Female:* Suave! Yeah, we're gon-na *Both:* bop, bop, bop, bop to the top;

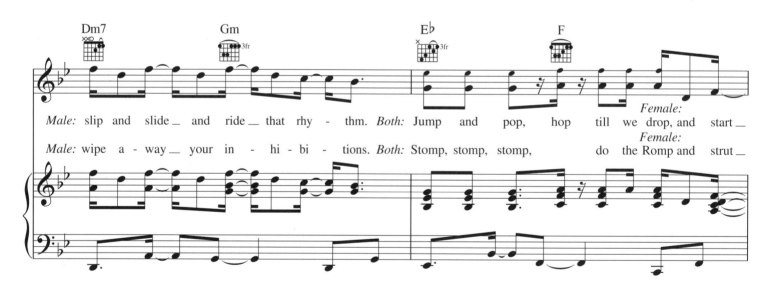

Male: slip and slide ___ and ride ___ that rhy-thm. *Both:* Jump and pop, hop till we drop, and start *Female:*

Male: wipe a-way ___ your in-hi-bi-tions. *Both:* Stomp, stomp, stomp, do the Romp and strut ___ *Female:*

____ a-gain. ___ *Both:* Zip, zap, zop, flop like a mop;

____ your stuff. ___ *Both:* Bop, bop, bop, straight to the top;

To Coda

Male: scoot a - round __ the cor - ner. __ Both: Move it to the groove __ till the mu - sic
Male: go - ing for __ the glor - y. __ Both: We'll keep step - ping up, __ and we just won't

stops. __ Do the bop, bop, bop to the top;

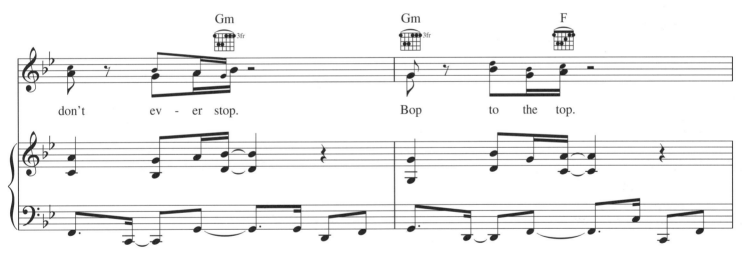

don't ev - er stop. Bop to the top.

Gim - me, gim - me; shim-my, shim-my. Shake some boot - y and turn a - round. __

Flash a smile in their di - rec - tion.

D.S. al Coda

Female: Show some mus - cle. *Male:* Do the hus - tle. *Female:* Yeah, we're gon - na

CODA

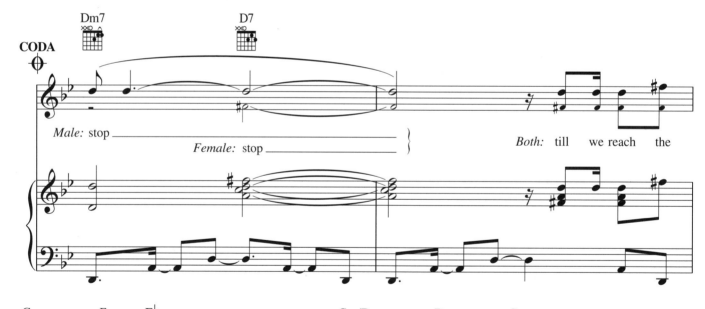

Male: stop

Female: stop

Both: till we reach the

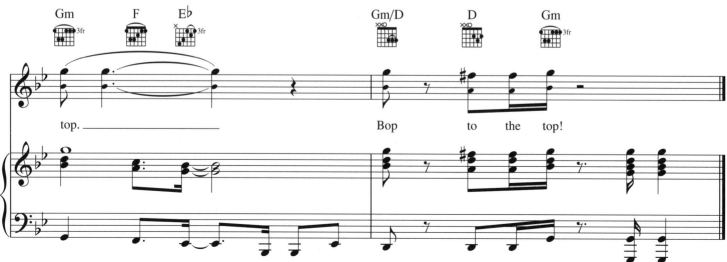

top. Bop to the top!

BREAKING FREE

Words and Music by
JAMIE HOUSTON

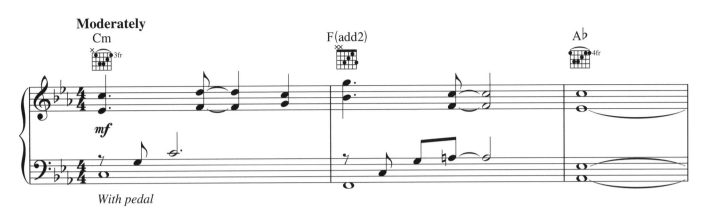

Moderately

With pedal

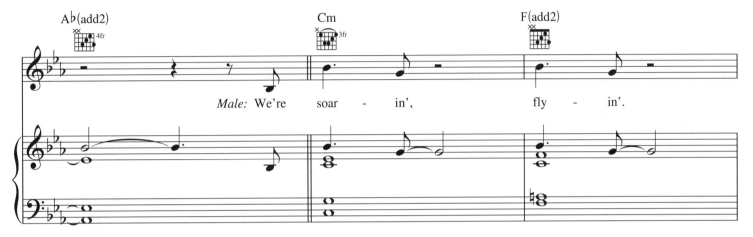

Male: We're soar - in', fly - in'.

There's not a star in heav - en that we can't reach. *Female:* If we're try -

- in', _____ so we're break - in' free.

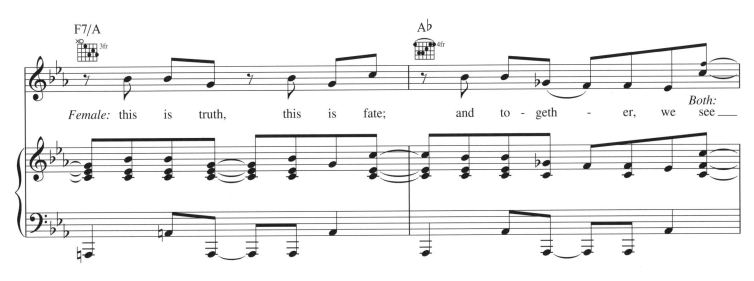

WE'RE ALL IN THIS TOGETHER

Words and Music by MATTHEW GERRARD
and ROBBIE NEVIL

Moderately

All: To - geth - er, to - geth - er, to - geth - er, ev - 'ry - one.
All: To - geth - er, we're there __ for each oth - er ev - 'ry time.

To - geth - er, to - geth - er, c' - mon, __ let's have some fun.
To - geth - er, to - geth - er,

c' - mon, __ let's do this right.
Male: Here and now, __ it's
Male: We're all here, __ and

Recorded a half step lower.

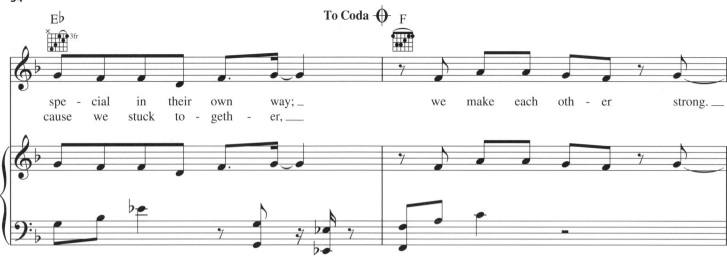

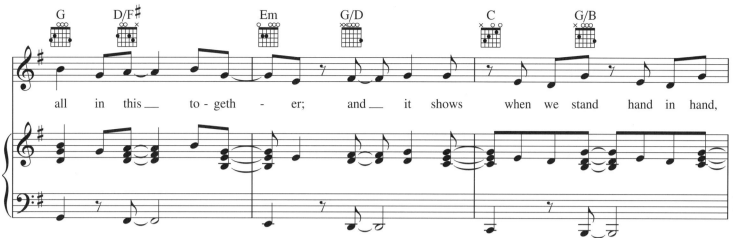

all in this __ to - geth - er; and __ it shows when we stand hand in hand,

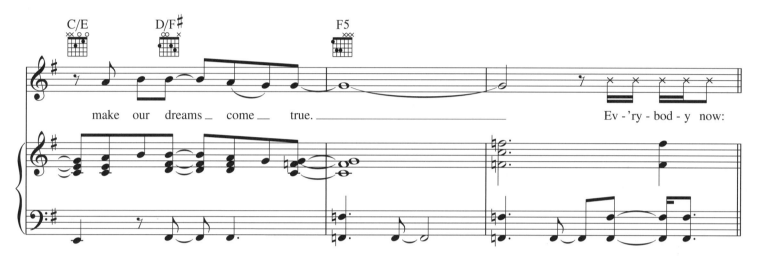

make our dreams __ come __ true. _____ Ev -'ry - bod - y now:

To - geth - er, to - geth - er, to - geth - er, ev -'ry - one.
To - geth - er, we're there __ for each oth - er ev -'ry time.

To - geth - er, to - geth - er, c' - mon, __ let's have some fun.
To - geth - er, to - geth - er,

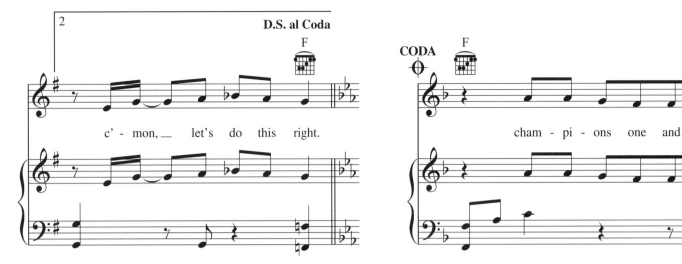

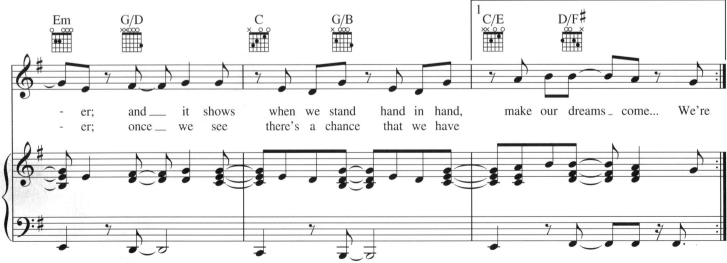

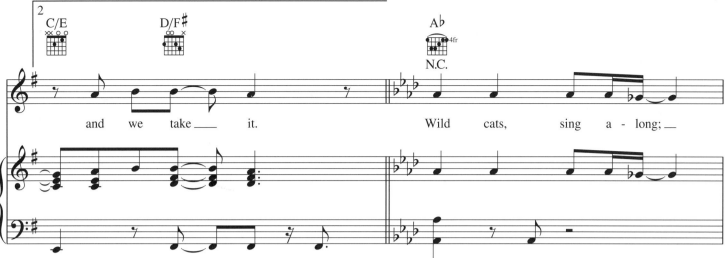

and we take ___ it. Wild cats, sing a - long; _

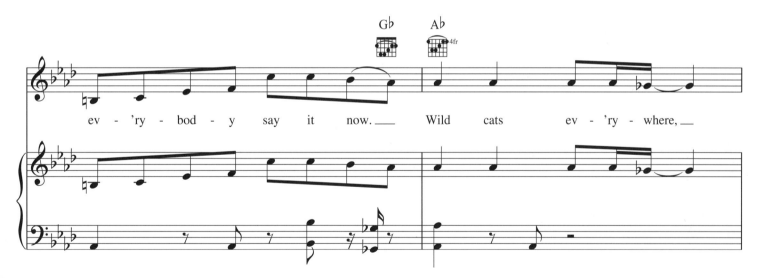

yeah, you real - ly got it go - in' on. __ Wild cats in the house; _

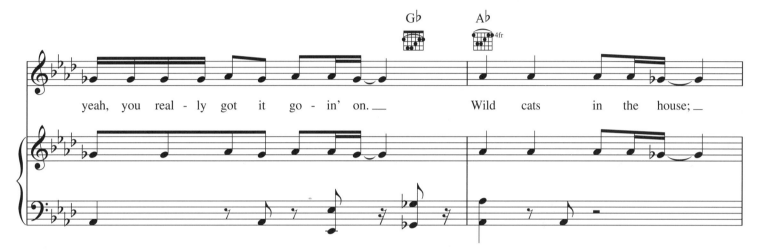

ev - 'ry - bod - y say it now. __ Wild cats ev - 'ry - where, _

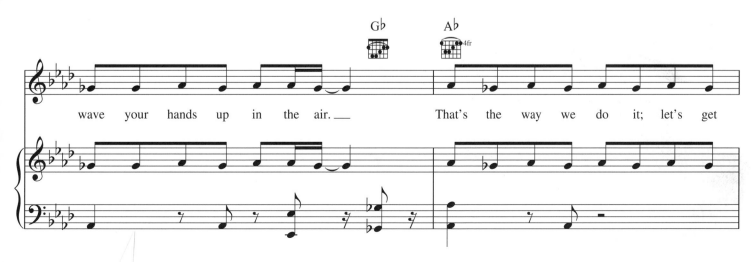

wave your hands up in the air. __ That's the way we do it; let's get

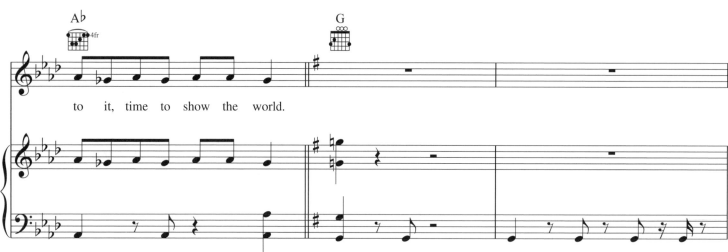

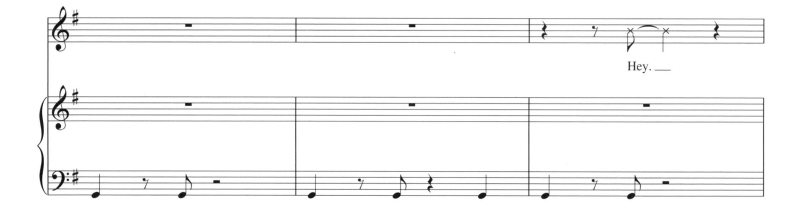

and we see ___ that. We're all in this ___ to-geth-er; and ___ it shows
we can make ___ it. We're all in this ___ to-geth-er; once ___ we see

when we stand hand in hand, make our dreams ___ come... We're
there's a chance that we have, and we take ___ it.

Wild cats ev-'ry-where, ___ wave your hands up in the air. ___

That's the way we do it; let's get to it, c'-mon ___ ev-'ry-one! ___

I CAN'T TAKE MY EYES OFF OF YOU

Words and Music by MATTHEW GERRARD
and ROBBIE NEVIL

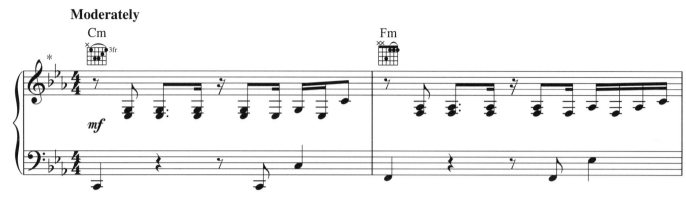

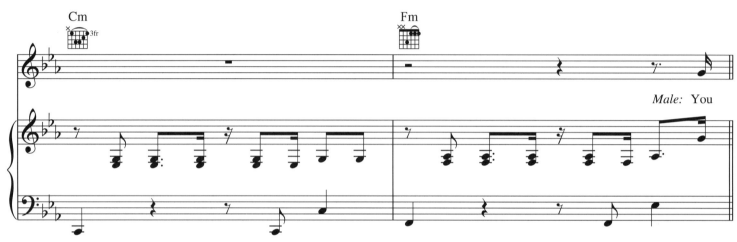

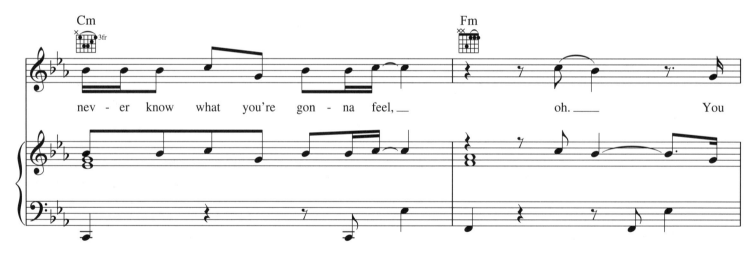

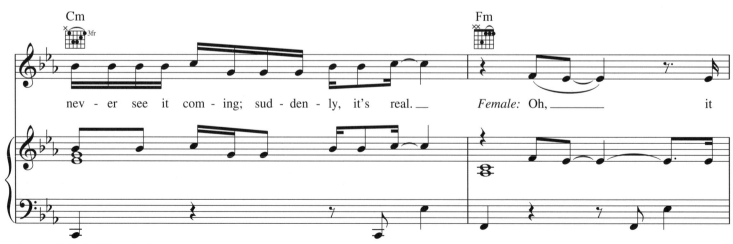

*Recorded a half step higher.

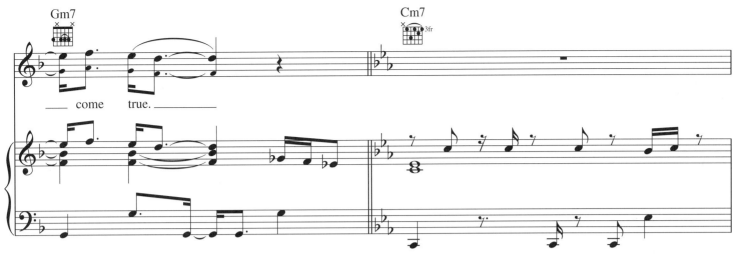

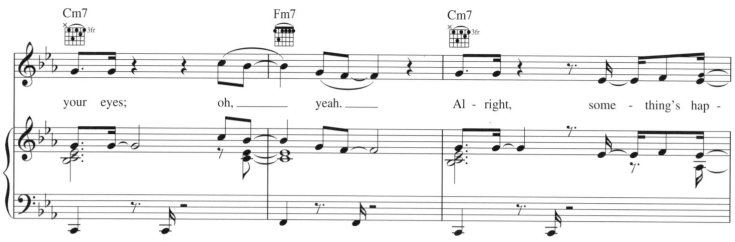

your eyes; oh, _____ yeah. _____ Al - right, some - thing's hap -

- pen - ing, __ 'cause ev - 'ry - one's_ a - round, but you're_ the on -

- ly one __ I see. __ I can't take my eyes off of you. __
can't take my eyes off of you; __

I know you feel the same way, too. __
feel - ings like I nev - er knew. __